Trust

Julie Murray

Abdo
CHARACTER EDUCATION
Kids

abdopublishing.com

Published by Abdo Kids, a division of ABDO, PO Box 398166, Minneapolis, Minnesota 55439.
Copyright © 2018 by Abdo Consulting Group, Inc. International copyrights reserved in all countries.
No part of this book may be reproduced in any form without written permission from the publisher.

Printed in the United States of America, North Mankato, Minnesota.

052017

092017

THIS BOOK CONTAINS
RECYCLED MATERIALS

Photo Credits: iStock, Shutterstock

Production Contributors: Teddy Borth, Jennie Forsberg, Grace Hansen

Design Contributors: Christina Doffing, Candice Keimig, Dorothy Toth

Publisher's Cataloging in Publication Data

Names: Murray, Julie, 1969-, author.

Title: Trust / by Julie Murray.

Description: Minneapolis, Minnesota : Abdo Kids, 2018 | Series: Character
education | Includes bibliographical references and index.

Identifiers: LCCN 2016962335 | ISBN 9781532100130 (lib. bdg.) |
ISBN 9781532100826 (ebook) | ISBN 9781532101373 (Read-to-me ebook)

Subjects: LCSH: Trust--Juvenile literature. | Trust in children--Juvenile literature. |
Children--Conduct of life--Juvenile literature. | Social skills in
children--Juvenile literature.

Classification: DDC 179/.9--dc23

LC record available at http://lccn.loc.gov/2016962335

Table of Contents

Trust

Trust is all around us.

Do you see it?

4

Pedro talks to his dad.

He tells the truth.

Lola raises her hand. Her teacher trusts her to follow rules.

Evan takes a test. He does his own work. He does not **cheat**.

Zack gives back the money he found. He does not take it.

Hui helps his mom. She trusts him to do a good job.

Jane keeps her **promises**.
She does what she says
she would do.

Ana takes out the garbage.
Her parents trust her to do
her chores.

Were you trusted today?

Some Ways to Be Trusted

Do Your Chores

Follow the Rules

Help Others

Tell the Truth

Glossary

cheat
to break the rules in a dishonest way.

promise
a statement that something will be done.

chore
a common task around the house or yard.

Index

abdokids.com

Use this code to log on to abdokids.com and access crafts, games, videos, and more!

Abdo Kids Code:
CTK0130